Peace

Facing Illness with Faith

FR. PATRICK RITTER

Liguori

Imprimi Potest: Stephen T. Rehrauer, CSsR, Provincial
Denver Province, the Redemptorists

Published by Liguori Publications, Liguori, Missouri 63057
To order, visit Liguori.org or call 800-325-9521.

Library of Congress Cataloging-in-Publication Data

Names: Ritter, Patrick, author.
Title: Profound peace : facing illness with faith / Fr. Patrick Ritter.
Description: Liguori : Liguori Publications, 2018.
Identifiers: LCCN 2018036795 | ISBN 9780764828119
Subjects: LCSH: Sick—Religious life. | Ritter, Pat. | Catholic
    Church—Clergy—Biography. | Priests—Washington (State)
    —Biography.
Classification: LCC BV4910 .R58 2018 | DDC 248.8/6092 [B] —dc23
LC record available at https://lccn.loc.gov/2018036795

ISBN 978-0-7648-2811-9

Liguori Publications, a nonprofit corporation, is an apostolate of
the Redemptorists. To learn more about the Redemptorists, visit
Redemptorists.com.

Cover image: Shutterstock

Printed in the United States of America
22 21 20 19 18 / 5 4 3 2 1
First Edition

Contents

Foreword

Many of us have faced the fear, uncertainty, vulnerability, loss of control, and pain that come with illness and surgery. While we may not have recognized it or admitted it beforehand, most of us had told ourselves for years that we were in charge of our lives and quite capable of fearlessly confronting whatever would come our way—and that we were supposed to live that way as adults.

However, life and its unexpected turns have a way of changing perspective on our many assumptions. Illness not only brings physical suffering, it also causes us to change attitudinally, spiritually, and emotionally. Moreover, illness challenges us to seek and expect in earnest the kind of healing of body, attitude, soul, and emotion that God provides for us. The roads to healing are as varied as our histories and personalities, and God is eager to accompany us personally along the way. One of the first lessons God wants to teach us is that we are not alone and we shouldn't try to make it alone. God walks within and beside us, as do the many friends he sends to help us.

Fr. Pat Ritter's inviting book, *Profound Peace: Facing Illness with Faith,* is a gentle, sure, and wise guide along healing's path. In these pages, you'll soon see how his experience of multiple serious surgeries and complications opened him to God's love and healing in powerful, life-changing ways. In the midst of the challenges that life unexpectedly gave him, he found peace, courage, and even deeper faith. Active and creative as a busy pastor for many years, he let God teach him vital lessons through illness and surgery: to let go of control, trust in God's love, have confidence in the medical professionals caring for him, keep a positive attitude, learn to be vulnerable, rely on the loving help of family and friends, be open to surprises and the humor in each situation, stay close to God's word and sacraments of the Church, and grow even closer to Jesus in prayer.

Fr. Ritter discovered the foundation of prayer that had been part of his life for years not only brought stability and hope during his trials, it grew even stronger through those trials. In addition, his closeness to Jesus became even more palpable and life-sustaining.

Several years ago, Pope Francis said, "Fear is not a good counselor; he gives you bad advice." But, as Fr. Ritter puts it, "Fear does not have the last word. God does." Fear paralyzes, but God gives us the strength to put one foot in front of the other all the way to healing.

If you or a loved one have faced the unsettledness and disorientation of illness, this book will help you walk with God along a path that will bring you peace.

His peace,
Archbishop J. Peter Sartain, DD, STL
Archdiocese of Seattle

Acknowledgments

My sincere thanks to Archbishop J. Peter Sartain for his support of this project.

I greatly appreciate the work and wisdom of Julie Cipoletti, who served as my editor. Without her, this book would never have been published.

I am dedicating *Profound Peace* to my good friend, Fr. Gary Morelli, who died of cancer a few years ago. He was by my side through six surgeries.

Introduction

After answering God's call and enjoying the high energy and full life of serving as a priest in the Archdiocese of Seattle for more than forty years, everything suddenly changed for me.

The life I knew was turned upside down when I faced a series of five separate surgeries on my left hip, a life-threatening infection, and back surgery.

I was blessed to have some of the country's best doctors and medical care, a close and personal relationship with Jesus, and the support of family and my parish community. With their gifts and God's grace, I'm thankful to be here to share my story of experiencing a profound peace in the middle of a personal health crisis.

Are you facing health challenges today? My wish is that this book will help give you the assurance—deep in your heart—that you're not alone when facing the pain, suffering, and challenges involved in whatever your health crisis may be. God is with you on your journey. I believe that great hope from God will see you through to the other side of any health challenge.

If you spend much time with me, you'll find that I'm a storyteller at heart and love to share a good laugh.

One of my favorite stories involves an old Irish pastor who was just finishing a nuptial Mass for a young couple. Just before they kissed, he decided to give a short sermon. "Stop! You think you're going to live like Prince Charming and Cinderella. Well, let me tell you, you're not!"

And then he went on to describe so many things that can happen in a marriage, like losing a job or having to move. You may get sick yourself, but you can't stay in bed because the children need you. The children will get measles or chicken pox.

I wondered why he was telling them all this when they were so starry-eyed and just starting out, having just pledged to love one another "in good times and in bad, in sickness and in health." But I will never forget what he said next.

"Yes, you're going to have problems like everyone else. But it's how you choose to *deal* with your problems in life that will make all the difference! Now kiss and get out of here!"

And so it is with my experience of facing surgery and illness with faith. You have to face and deal with your difficulties when they arise, knowing that God is with you and suffers right along with you through your journey.

I hope this book will help you along the way and lead you to the beautiful experience of a profound peace.

I'll be praying for you.

God bless,
Fr. Pat

If you have specific prayer intentions you'd like to send to Fr. Pat, please e-mail his team at PrayerRequestsFrPat@outlook.com and Fr. Pat will be happy to include your requests in his prayers.

Chapter One

Life Can Quickly Take a Shocking Turn

*Even though I walk through the valley of the
shadow of death, I will fear no evil,
for you are with me.*

PSALM 23:4

At sixty-four, I was running a vibrant parish in a
high-growth area of suburban Seattle and had my future planned. I would retire in about three years and
spend part of my time living in sunny Palm Desert,
CA. I had worked with the people of the parish and
finished a major building project that would serve
generations of families to come. My condo was just
about paid off. Everything was on track, and I was
feeling great.

Then one day I began to drag my left leg. I
thought perhaps I had sprained it at the gym the day
before. But over the next ten days it got worse, to the

point that some friends took me to the emergency unit. I couldn't walk at all. The doctor wasn't sure what it was. Fortunately I had a priest friend who could cover the three weekend Masses for me. It was just before Thanksgiving, and people brought me so much turkey, I thought I was going to sprout feathers!

The next week I was taken to a specialist at the hospital who took x-rays of my left hip. "You have no cartilage left in your hip," he said. "Someday you probably will need surgery."

"I can't have this problem," I replied. "I'm only sixty-four!" Yet I failed to recall that my mother had hip surgery when she was sixty-two.

After discussing options with my physician, I decided on a cortisone injection to alleviate the pain so I could offer Christmas Masses at my parish. Under fluoroscopy by the interventional radiologist, I received the injection, and then my left leg starting trembling and raised up toward the ceiling. I asked the nurse, "What's it doing?"

"I don't know," she said. "I've never seen that happen."

In a minute it settled down, but then it really began to hurt. I had worked with a trainer at the gym for five years. During that time, apparently the muscles in the left leg had all pulled to the right trying to protect the hip. Now that they were relaxing they didn't know how to cooperate with each other. All the muscles in the leg hurt. The pain was so intense, I called the doctor and asked if he had time in the next few days to perform surgery! We arranged for surgery in four days. My only personal experience with surgery was fifty-nine years earlier, when I had my tonsils removed as a kindergartner.

I was concerned about my parochial responsibilities, but fortunately I had secured excellent staff members who were more than capable of handling all that was involved in running our lively parish and school. I felt matters would be in good hands, but little did I know how my life would change.

My doctors told me that the greatest fear is the fear of the unknown. Isn't that the truth? I knew I needed God's help to get me through this. I received the anointing of the sick and felt an overwhelming sense of support and love as the parish and school staff gathered to pray for me. I would soon discover that my journey through surgery and illness had only just begun. What I did know was that I had the undeniable sense that God was with me, by my side.

Prayer

(while lighting a candle or vigil light)
*God our Savior, allow me to follow your holy light
and to trust that you are leading me along your path.
Enlighten my tough decisions and burn away from me
any resistance to your will.*

Reminder

*Life doesn't always follow the path you have set for
yourself.*

Reflection

*Reflect on the shock of a time when your life may have
been turned upside down. Where did you see glimmers
of God's light illuminating your darkness, leading you
along the way?*

Chapter Two

A Setback and Experiencing a Miracle

I believe I shall see the LORD's goodness
in the land of the living.

PSALM 27:13

I was in the hospital four days and then in a nursing facility for five. When I was preparing to go home, I noticed this foul-smelling stuff oozing from my wound. When I arrived home I called the doctor and told him there was something terribly wrong. An ambulance took me back to the hospital, and my physician returned me to the operating room where my hip was debrided and irrigated around the titanium artificial joint, and multiple bacterial cultures were taken.

The culture grew in two days instead of four. It was MRSA (methicillin-resistant *Staphylococcus aureus*), which is a difficult type of deep staph infection. I had no idea what MRSA was or where it came from. It is a very dangerous infection that can cause death, and is often associated with invasive procedures such as artificial joint surgery. MRSA was a big story on the news at the time. It was called a superbug because it's resistant to many of the antibiotics used to treat ordinary staph infections.

The doctor moved quickly the next day, took out the titanium hip, and put a spacer inside my body where my hip joint had been. It was made of metal and cement loaded with antibiotics to fight the infection.

But then the next day, my team of physicians recommended another surgery because the cultures still showed traces of MRSA deep inside my thigh bone, or femur. I didn't feel sick, but I knew it was dangerous. "I've had a wonderful life as a priest," I said. "If this is it, this is it! But I don't think so. I'll be sound asleep, so you go right ahead."

I knew I needed to ask God to get me through this, so I called on a friend I had known for forty years to help me pray before the fourth surgery began.

I had practiced contemplative prayer for many years and knew what I needed to do. We prayed together, and then I entered a very deep and quiet place in my soul.

After about forty minutes I began to be filled with profound peace that seemed to fill every cell in my body, from head to toe. I had never experienced anything like it before. I noticed something beginning to happen. I was experiencing a vision of some sort. Even though I knew I was in the hospital room because I occasionally opened one eye, I felt I was in another room with a white floor and no walls. I sat there quietly, and within ten minutes sensed the presence of MRSA in the right side of the room. It wasn't a person, and it didn't feel threatening, but it was a manifestation. I sensed it much like one would if you walked into a totally dark room and then you eventually felt through a sixth sense that someone was sitting there. I wasn't afraid. I just found the vision fascinating.

Then, in a few minutes, I could feel the presence of God. The presence was behind my left shoulder and above my head. Once I realized who it was, I asked one question: "Is it MRSA or me?"

"MRSA will die and you will live," God said. When the vision was over, I opened my eyes. I didn't want to tell my friend what had happened because I hadn't absorbed it yet, so I asked if anything was different after we prayed.

"There was a wonderful peace which filled the room," my friend said. God was faithful and provided profound peace in the middle of my health crisis. When I became more aware of what had happened, I realized that this overwhelming peace was something I had never felt before, a great gift from God.

Within a few hours, the fourth surgery began. I found out later that a close priest friend, Fr. Gary Morelli, had asked the doctor how things went. The doctor said he was waiting to see how I would make it through the recovery period and the long infection-control process that would determine my future function.

God's profound peace remained with me, and I knew that I was experiencing nothing short of a miracle.

Prayer

God our Father, you conquer the darkness by the light of your word. Strengthen within our hearts the faith you have given us. I ask this in the name of Jesus. Amen.

Reminder

You may experience a wall, but it's not the end.

Reflection

What aspect of your health challenges can you hand over to God in prayer? Every experience is unique, but have you taken the hand of God in prayer?

Chapter Three

We All Need a Christian Community

What will separate us from the love of Christ? ...No, in all things we conquer overwhelmingly through him who loved us.

ROMANS 8:35, 37

When it was time for my fourth surgery, people arrived at the church late at night to pray for my health after learning I was in the medical fight of my life. It was the Christmas season, and there was no way for me in a short time to get out the news of my latest medical challenge and do it in an accurate manner.

Instead, I asked Fr. Morelli, the priest covering for me at Mass, to read a statement before each of the Christmas Eve and Christmas Day liturgies.

In the statement, I explained the surgeries and told the congregants I had contracted MRSA. I implored them for their prayers. (I was later told that there was a gasp, then a hush throughout the stunned congregation.) It wasn't the ideal way to begin a joyful Christmas celebration, but I wanted to share my journey with our faith community in an honest, transparent way, and rely on the power of their prayers.

It was seven weeks before I could return to the church and concelebrate Mass. I will never forget the reception I received, people clapping and cheering as I came up the ramp in a wheelchair to enter the church. How wonderful people were in their love and support!

Yes, now that man who had gone to the gym for many years and was the leader of the parish was exceptionally vulnerable, being pushed in a wheelchair by somebody else. It was a very emotional experience but one that I accepted.

I felt the love of all on that special day. It was the best day of my life next to my ordination day. Without a supportive community, it's very difficult to face these moments in our lives. I consider myself very fortunate to have such a loving, Christian community.

Prayer

Father, you illumine the night and bring the dawn to scatter the darkness. Let us pass through this night in safety, rising when morning comes to give you thanks and praise. We long to look upon your face where night will be no more, nor will we need light from lamp or sun, for you shall give us light, and we shall reign forever and ever (see Revelation 22:4–5).

Reminder

Without people of faith to support you, life becomes very difficult indeed.

Reflection

Think about who your personal community might be. Is it your parish? Your school? Family? Office staff? A combination of these people? Let them know when you need help and ask them to keep you in prayer. Our faith communities are here to support us, as no one can go through life alone. If you don't have a faith community, now is a great time to find one.

Chapter Four

Home Sweet
(Upside Down) Home

Making Peace With
My New Reality

[Jesus said,] "Everything that the Father gives me will come to me, and I will not reject anyone who comes to me, because I came down not to do my own will but the will of the one who sent me."

JOHN 6:37–38

When it was time to come home from the hospital, I discovered that my "home sweet home" had been turned upside down to accommodate my wheelchair and temporary lack of mobility.

My comforts of home didn't look or feel like I remembered. My recliner had been pushed into a corner. Due to my hip, I could sit in only one straight-back chair. I was used to an orderly home, and now things were a big mess! The rugs had been rolled up in a corner. There were 300 unanswered letters and cards piled on my dining-room table. The peaceful home environment I remembered was now just a memory.

I could easily have become irritated, but as my father would have said, "What's the point of being angry? It's a waste of energy. You have a choice. Either you deal with the situation or it will deal with you." I also remembered St. Paul's words, "Be angry, but do not sin; do not let the sun set on your anger, and do not leave room for the devil" (Ephesians 4:26–27).

So I started taking charge of my situation and making peace with my new reality, knowing that my health challenges weren't going away anytime soon. I'd be in a wheelchair for a long time and then use a walker for five months until the MRSA was dead. Then I'd be ready for my fifth surgery, where doctors would give me a new titanium hip.

People who've been incapacitated know the challenges involved, especially if they were used to living alone and always being independent, like I was. I had to learn how to shower using a special bench that fit over the tub. I couldn't put all my weight on my left leg—only about fifty pounds. It was difficult to shave, so I bought an electric razor. Everything seemed to take three times as long. I had to have someone come in and make my bed because

I couldn't lift anything. I learned patience, which was difficult for me.

Fortunately my sister, Jean, was a great help. She came and stayed with me throughout those initial days. It's strange how your world changes. A week later, after Jean returned home, I kept a light on at night to help me pretend that someone was there. It made me feel safer.

I had to learn how to get out of bed differently; how to put on my clothes in bed. I put on my shoes with the help of a special shoehorn.

I had good days and bad days, and I had to deal with each one differently. I found that writing down the small things that I had accomplished each day helped me move toward healing and recovery.

I could've felt sorry for myself with one challenge after another and asked, "Why me?" But there's no answer to that question. We are dealt different sets of cards. Life happens, and it's how we deal with life, with God by our side, that makes all the difference. Imagine trying to do this without God accompanying you through it all!

Prayer

Lord, free me from this dark night. Let the light of your resurrection dawn within our hearts to bring us the radiance of eternal life.

Reminder

Sometimes our lives seem shattered, but from those pieces we discover a new reality.

Reflection

Picture in your mind your "home sweet home" before you arrive back from the hospital. Be open to the idea that things won't feel exactly like they did before. Ask God to help you make peace with the new reality as God guides you through this transition.

Chapter Five

Another Setback and More Transitions

I praise you, LORD, for you raised me up
and did not let my enemies rejoice over me.

PSALM 30:2

I had two months of antibiotics to kill the MRSA. Fortunately, a retired nurse from the parish came by to administer the antibiotic. It took about forty-five minutes a day. Then I had an allergic reaction to the medication. I broke out in hives and ended up going back to the specialist. The doctor prescribed another antibiotic, but this one took two hours to administer each day. But what could I do? This would be my life for a while. When people asked me how I was doing, I would try to be honest with them. I've found that it's not good to overly complain about personal struggles, but neither is it advisable to say everything is fine when it's not.

I was stricken by sheer boredom during that

time. It seemed like so much of my time was being wasted before the final surgery five months down the road. I still offered Mass and preached, but now I was celebrating Mass from a wheelchair. I could only work a few hours each day.

When the MRSA was totally gone, I had the fifth surgery. Then physical therapy began in earnest. Just walking a flight of stairs again was a huge deal. A man in the parish took me to all my doctor's appointments and multiple physical therapy sessions. I was very fortunate.

One thing I discovered is that physical therapy really hurts! Don't kid yourself. I had to learn to walk all over again, and it was scary. It took a long time, but I'm grateful to the therapists who worked with me and encouraged me along the way.

I did my exercises as prescribed. I had a limp but was determined not to live my life with one. Eventually the limp went away, and I was walking better with a walker, then a cane. Finally I was able to walk on my own. I deeply appreciated all the phone calls and letters of support I received. It's amazing how our family and faith community contributed to my healing through their care and support.

It was humbling to have to learn to accept help. I had to learn to ask for assistance in shopping for meals, in going to my appointments, in doing many of the household chores in my condo. I had to be so careful not to fall because I wasn't sure if I would have been able to get up. Now I wear a medical alert button at night, which gives me a sense of peace and security through the evening hours.

What I could no longer control, I eventually surrendered to others and to God. In that surrender was an intense experience of Christ's promise, "Peace I leave with you; my peace I give to you" (John 14:27).

Prayer

Lord God, source of all compassion, fill my heart with thanksgiving. Let me be an example for others in their struggles.

Reminder

Fear does not have the last word. God does.

Reflection

Decide to take care of yourself. Be good to yourself, and do what's needed to properly heal. Praise God for all the little and big steps toward recovery. He is with you every step of the way.

Chapter Six

Making Peace with a Lack of Control

LORD, hear my prayer;
in your faithfulness listen to my pleading.

PSALM 143:1

"Illness and suffering have always been among the gravest problems confronted in human life. In illness, man experiences his powerlessness, his limitations, and his finitude. Every illness can make us glimpse death. Illness can lead to anguish, self-absorption, sometimes even despair and revolt against God. It can also make a person more mature, helping him discern in his life what is not essential so that he can turn toward that which is. Very often illness provokes a search for God and a return to him" (*Catechism of the Catholic Church*, 1500–1501).

It was becoming clear I could no longer control my destiny. Now I knew that I never could. This was so hard to accept at first. I had prearranged my future, but I finally learned to let go of my plans and let God manifest his will. What's the old saying? "Man plans and God laughs."

But God makes beautiful things out of our suffering. We only need to open our eyes and look around so we don't miss the beauty. Illnesses and surgeries can bring families closer together. I am so grateful for my sister, brother-in-law, nieces, and cousins who called or came to visit.

My impatient mind may have become very unrealistic about my situation and wanted my body to heal faster than it could. My healing body would respond by saying, "That's a great idea, but we're not doing it! But keep those ideas coming! And where would you like the pain today?"

I decided it would be good to learn to be kind to myself during this long journey back to health. Often I would decide to take the day off and pretend I was on vacation, although I still did my exercises and kept up my regular prayer life.

I had to decide to make peace with taking care of myself and to taking the time to properly heal. This is tough for a type A personality. I was so accustomed to being in charge. Now I had become very vulnerable. Perhaps this new mindset was a gift. I often tell people surgery or illness is not the worst that can happen. Having no faith to deal with these realities is the worst.

I also took comfort in these words of St. Francis de Sales: "Do not look forward to what might happen tomorrow; the same Everlasting Father who cares for you today, will take care of you tomorrow and every day. Either he will shield you from suffering or he will give you unfailing strength to bear it. Be at peace, then, and put aside all anxious thoughts and imaginings."

Prayer

Lord, let fear not take over my life, but rather may the peace that you alone can bring be mine this day. Mary, my Mother, help me say what you told God—"Your will be done"—despite the uncertainty in knowing what God has in mind for me.

Reminder

Control is not real. It just feels that way, when we lack trust in God. Trust in God is real.

Reflection

Close your eyes and spend time with God, releasing your worries about your situation into his hands. Thank God for the faith to take you through this challenging season of your life.

Chapter Seven

Stay Close to Christ Through Prayer All Your Life

The human heart plans the way,
but the LORD directs the steps.

PROVERBS 16:9

In 1969, I left the seminary after eight years of formation. I wasn't a priest yet. It was a confusing time because of the war in Vietnam and Cambodia, and much political unrest in the world.

I entered the seminary out of my love of liturgy and music, but I soon discovered that wasn't enough. I needed something more. So I left and became a teacher in the public schools. It wasn't that I didn't want to be a priest, but I wanted to ask God what he wanted of me from the gift of my life.

After teaching all day and preparing lesson plans for the next day I would spend time each evening in quiet prayer, often not saying a word—just listening. After two years I discovered a wonderful personal relationship with Jesus. It has been the bedrock of my life ever since.

On December 8, 1972, I called the vocations office of the archdiocese and told them I felt God had asked me to be a priest, and I said yes. I have been happy as a priest for more than forty years. It hasn't always been easy, but what in life always is? Yet if we develop a relationship with Jesus, it will help us through anything. The Church has changed so much over those many years, but my prayer life has been the rudder that has guided me every moment in my life.

I recommend to others to stay close to Christ; to spend time in prayer each day and try to listen with your heart, not your mind. Often when times are good, people tend not to pray. But when times get tough (which will happen for all of us), when life has brought us to our knees, we really discover what prayer is all about.

Here's an exercise I ask people to do when I lead retreats. Draw a line on a piece of paper and put the number one on one end of the line and your present age on the other. Label tens, twenties, and so on, along the line. Then mark the major events of your life at different intervals—both the good and the challenging. Put good times above the line and the challenging times below the line. Now ask yourself when you felt closest to God. I can say with some certainty it's when you experienced difficulty that you felt closest to God. So why not pray every day to him so that you are prepared for these highs and lows of your life?

Psalm 139 helps us feel close to God: "LORD, you have probed me, you know me: you know when I sit and stand; you understand my thoughts from afar. You sift through my travels and my rest; with all my ways you are familiar. Even before a word is on my tongue, LORD, you know it all. Behind and before you encircle me and rest your hand upon me" (Psalm 139:1–5).

I have made prayer the most important part of my day. I make a strong pot of coffee when I get up. Then, before doing my personal grooming for the day, I pray the morning prayer of the Church and just open my heart to God for a while. I encourage people to do this opening-of-the-heart prayer for ten minutes each day, at the same time, in the same chair. Don't do more than this. Eventually you'll find yourself taken somewhere else, and you will lose track of time. But that's OK because you've entered more deeply into your relationship with Jesus. He'll guide you in all ways and in all days.

God doesn't care what form of prayer you use as long as you spend time with him every day. It's

very important to stop talking all the time and spend time listening. This is called contemplative prayer. If you're talking all the time, you can't hear what God has in mind for you.

I knew that when I faced these surgeries, together God and I could face anything. He probed me and he knows me! My emotions were all over the place: fear, anger, helplessness, and so on. But at a very deep level I felt a real peace and calm due to many years of my relationship with Jesus. It's only with that deep experience of faith and peace that you can handle anything that confronts you in life. I often felt when I was younger that I could do it alone, but I couldn't. Life was too challenging. I needed Jesus.

Prayer

Lord, watch over me by day and by night. In the midst of life's challenges, strengthen me with your never-changing love.

Reminder

Together Christ and I can handle anything, although the obstacles may feel insurmountable at times.

Reflection

Commit to starting your days with Jesus in quiet, contemplative prayer. Decide to invite Jesus to guide your life and truly listen with an open heart. "In the morning let me hear of your mercy, for in you I trust. Show me the path I should walk, for I entrust my life to you" (Psalm 143:8).

Chapter Eight

God's Gift of a Positive Attitude Is Everything!

He took away our infirmities
and bore our diseases.

MATTHEW 8:17; SEE ISAIAH 53:4

When you're facing surgery or illness, a determined and positive attitude is essential. Your whole mind, soul, and spirit will take notice. They will work together for your good. The doctors, surgeries, and medications are not enough. Developing a positive attitude is fundamental. If you just accept your situation and let doctors do their work, you are missing one important factor—yourself. You become resigned to your situation. You must say to yourself, "I'm going to handle this and work through it. No one else can do it for me."

It is said that attitude is just as powerful as any surgery or medicine because the mind, soul, and body have their own system of handling any situation. God put these systems in us, and we have only to believe in them and use them for healing. You can handle anything with the right attitude!

God always gives us the grace to approach any situation. We all have a purpose in life, and God will not be content until that purpose is fulfilled. But you have to do your part as well. Never give in when difficulties come. Most of us are far more resilient in the face of adversity than we ever imagine. Know you have the ability, while holding God's hand, to face them. When you live long enough, you will see how his gentle hand guided your life along the way. He blocked the wrong paths, encouraged the right decisions, and put people into our lives to help us.

But you have to make a decision to handle your situation, whatever that is, and then your whole world will begin to change for the better. Live just one day at a time and put one foot forward as you handle your situation. Take the next best step in front of you, and God will show you the way.

Saint Augustine used to say, "Pray as though everything depended on God. Work as though everything depended on you." Between those two, everything works together for the best.

Prayer

Give me the grace, courage, and determination to face whatever comes my way with a loving heart.

Reminder

If you don't handle your difficult situations, they will handle you.

Reflection

Thank God for his gift of a positive outlook. Ask Jesus to help you take advantage of this gift in this season of your life.

Chapter Nine

Celebrating the Sacraments of Unity, Healing, and His Holy Word

*The LORD is my light and my salvation;
whom should I fear?*

PSALM 27:1

Celebrating the holy Eucharist and listening to God's divine word will keep you centered and nourished through the many ups and downs of life. You will be strengthened as you are unified with all the faithful throughout the world.

I believe it's a huge mistake to stop going to the Eucharist. We think we can live life on our own, but we can't. When the winds of destruction hit us, we're often not strong enough to withstand them. We have to develop spiritual strength much like when we strengthen our bodies. The holy Eucharist was celebrated for the first time at the Last Supper and has been a gift to us ever since. It is "bread for the journey."

"Is anyone among you sick? He should summon the presbyters of the church and they should pray over him and anoint [him] with oil in the name of the Lord, and the prayer of faith will save the sick person, and the Lord will raise him up. If he has committed any sins, he will be forgiven" (James 5:14–15). I believe the anointing of the sick is one of the most powerful sacraments we have. I've seen miracles happen in the most difficult of situations. The Second Vatican Council brought back its original meaning as a sacrament of healing. When you are about to go into surgery or have discovered you have an illness, call your local priest or the hospital chaplain and have yourself anointed. I did that when I went into surgery. What I experienced within hours was a deep sense of peace and hope as Christ came to me in a very special way—a way like no other.

I also read holy Scripture every day. You don't have to be a Scripture scholar to do so. Just read it slowly and let it speak to your heart. If there's one particular word that speaks to you, stop and ponder that word. God is saying something important to you.

Prayer

Lord God, give me a share in the life and love that your Spirit brings.

Reminder

Your burden will be light, for God is pulling with you.

Reflection

The Eucharist is God's greatest healing gift for us. Take advantage of the spiritual strength God offers through the treasure of the Holy Eucharist.

"May the receiving of your Body and Blood,
Lord Jesus Christ,
not bring me to judgment and condemnation,
but through your loving mercy
be for me protection in mind and body
and a healing remedy."

(PRIESTLY PRAYER BEFORE
COMMUNION AT MASS, FROM *ROMAN MISSAL*)

Chapter Ten

Five Years Later

Another Surgery with Lessons Learned

*So, as you received Christ Jesus the Lord,
walk in him...as you were taught, abounding in
thanksgiving.*

COLOSSIANS 2:6–7

About eighteen months ago I noticed that as I celebrated Mass, I started to use my cane again because the pain in my back was so severe. I almost fell a few times during the Eucharist.

I had gone to chiropractors, physical therapists, and acupuncturists over the years. Their treatments gave temporary relief, but nothing solved the problem of my back pain, which has existed for more than two decades. I was determined not to spend the rest of my life in a wheelchair. I would celebrate the holy Eucharist for as long as I could.

So I asked for an MRI and went to see a spine

surgeon. He discovered that two of my lower vertebrae were pushing against each other, creating extreme pain and instability. I wanted to do all I could so that physically, I could continue to offer Mass. After our consultation, I asked for surgery.

I prepared for surgery for a full month because I had learned so much from my previous surgeries. I had to prepare myself physically, mentally, emotionally, and spiritually. Again I had the best medical professionals caring for me. They were excellent. My sister came to help me, and I felt so grateful for the support of family and our faith community.

This time I depended even more on my relationship with Christ. In prayer I felt called by him to write this book to help others. Today I am pain free. I enjoy playing the piano again, visiting with friends, and offering the sacraments. God is so good and carries us through it all.

I'm grateful for this journey, as painful as it has been. It's not what I expected, but a new door opened to me showing more clearly God's care and love for me in all circumstances.

Over the years I've learned so much about faith, Christian community, a positive attitude, the sacraments, the best doctors, and my close relationship to Christ. I hope my story of facing surgery and illness with faith has helped you in some way toward finding profound peace.

Please know that you will remain in my personal prayers.

Prayer

Lord, my very existence is a gift from you. Let me live each day in gratitude.

Reminder

With God we can do anything.

Reflection

How will you prepare yourself physically, mentally, emotionally, and spiritually before your next surgery or health challenge? God will be with you all the way.

Epilogue

Was it perhaps a gift after all? I've often wondered. Did God plan these things to happen to me? I don't think so. Things just happen. But from these things that no one would ask to happen to them, people grow and one's life gains a new perspective, which includes acceptance.

I think this is what happened to me. I changed. I became more sensitive to people with disabilities because I had experienced what it's like to be in a wheelchair and to have limited mobility. My struggles required me to rely even more on God, so now I have the gift of a deeper faith than I did six years ago. Amazingly, I now experience no pain.

Today, I offer Mass while holding on to a four-pronged quad cane for stability, as my balance is still a struggle. I can't stand and give out holy Communion anymore at Mass, but people are understanding. They're glad that I'm there to offer the holy Eucharist and take care of them spiritually.

I often stop people I've never met who are using a walker or wheelchair and ask them how this happened. They're happy that someone asked them about their condition. I ask them their first name and tell them I'm a Catholic priest and that I'll be praying for them, which I do. I call people I know who are ill and ask them how they're doing. My surgeries have made me more sensitive to those who are suffering.

I often feel humbled now. Sometimes God does that for his own purposes. I shared this with a parishioner and he put it in perspective for me. "Father, don't feel so humbled," he said. "Half of the people in the parish walk with a cane. Now you can identify with them."

"My grace is sufficient for you, for power is made perfect in weakness," said the Lord to St. Paul. "I will rather boast most gladly of my weaknesses, in order that the power of Christ may dwell with me. Therefore, I am content with weaknesses… hardships…and constraints, for the sake of Christ; for when I am weak, then I am strong" (2 Corinthians 12:9–10).

I wonder if it's a gift that I experienced this, as a priest, so that I can better help people in my path reflect on how God is walking them through their own struggles, and holding them by the hand. Henri Nouwen's description of a "wounded healer" comes to mind.

So was it a gift after all? I still don't know, but while we can never be sure what God does for his own purposes, we can find a renewed sense of purpose in the experience.

"Son though he was, he learned obedience from what he suffered; and when he was made perfect, he became the source of eternal salvation for all who obey him, declared by God high priest according to the order of Melchizedek" (Hebrews 5:8–10).

God bless,
Fr. Pat

Finding a Smile in the Struggle

[Jesus said,] "Do not let your hearts be troubled.
You have faith in God; have faith also in me."

JOHN 14:1

When I look back at those times now, I remember so many lighthearted incidents that happened along the way:

- When I went in for therapy at the hospital for the first time, I saw a young man who just had knee surgery. I asked him what happened. He said he was in a motorcycle competition when he had an accident. But that wasn't the first time. He also had broken his arm, his left hand, and dislocated his shoulder. But he had to hurry up because he had another competition coming up. What a life!

- One time I was sound asleep in the hospital and could hear someone calling my name. I woke up to see this dark figure coming toward me at 2 in the morning. I didn't know it was the nurse. She hadn't turned the light on. There was only the light from the hallway. As she came closer, calling my name, I thought it was the angel of death coming to pick me up! I let out the most blood-curdling scream, and she ran from the room!

- My priest friend wanted to take me out for lunch when I was in the nursing facility. I asked him if his trunk was large enough for my wheelchair. He said we weren't going in the car but to the restaurant across the street. So he pushed me along the sidewalk, and every time he hit a crack in the pavement I felt a shock of pain go straight through my hip. It was November and seventeen degrees outside. We had a nice lunch and began the journey back. We were crossing a busy five-lane intersection when one of the large wheels on my wheelchair began to fall off! "I'm not going to die of MRSA," I yelled. "I'm going to be run over by a car!" He quickly reversed the wheelchair and pulled me backward over the curb as the light turned green!

- There was the time I had to be tested to see if the antibiotics had killed the MRSA. The hip joint is located deep inside the leg. It would be a procedure where two long needles of Novocain would first be inserted through the left leg to numb it, and then a larger one would be inserted into the hip joint. I knew I would probably faint, so I brought along a can of Coke to brace myself. The three nurses got me into a sterile gown, and the room was immaculate. When I opened the can of Coke, I didn't realize that I had shaken it up! The Coke spilt all over me and the floor. The nurses moved quickly to clean me and the surgery room. When the doctor came in, he asked, "Is everything sterile?" They responded, "It is now, doctor!"

Prayer

Lord, thank you for your many blessings. Give us strength to overcome our illnesses. Protect us, Lord. Gather us under the shadow of your wings and keep us as the apple of your eye.

Reminder

God has a sense of humor! Enjoy it!

Reflection

Where can you find a laughable moment or story in the situation you are going through? Finding a smile or laugh in your struggles can do wonders for the soul.

Appendix B

Prayers Before Surgery

I'm pleased to reprint the prayers and related text on pages 58-63, courtesy of my friends at Liguori Publications. I encourage those who are facing illness and surgery to join with friends and family to recite these prayers. My hope is that you also will experience God's amazing and profound peace.

The following prayer may be said by the patient before surgery:

Lord Jesus, I pray for your healing touch upon my body during my surgery. Guide the hands of the doctor and all who assist in the surgery. Use their skills to restore me to health and wholeness.

I ask you to remove any fear or anxiety from my mind and fill me with the peace that you alone can give. I place myself completely in your hands, Lord Jesus, trusting in your care and love for me. May my recovery be swift, my strength renewed, and my health restored.

Bless those, Lord, who are concerned about me today. I need their love and support and ask you to be with them in a special way. Replace any fear they have with your peace.

I place it all into your hands, Lord. You are the Divine Healer. Amen.

For this group prayer, gather around the bed of the person who will be entering surgery. Gently touch the person as you pray:

Leader: We call upon Jesus, our Lord and our Healer, to surround (name) with his healing power.

All: Lord, we know you are the one who heals. We ask you to place (name) under your protective and healing care. Remove any fear or anxiety from his/her spirit. Let your peace, Lord, abound in his/her body. As the time of surgery approaches, let him/her place all trust in you, Lord.

Leader: Our response is, "Into the Lord's hands we commend your body and spirit."

All: Into the Lord's hands we commend your body and spirit.

Leader: I lift my eyes to the mountains;
    where is help to come from?
Help comes to me from the Lord,
    who made heaven and earth!

(BASED ON PSALM 121)

All: Into the Lord's hands we commend your body and spirit.

Leader: The Lord will not let
     your footsteps slip.
He will guard you;
     he will not sleep!
The Lord will protect
     your comings and goings.

All: Into the Lord's hands we commend your body and spirit.

Leader: The Lord will guard and protect you.
The Lord will be a shade over you by day
     and a light for you by night.

All: Into the Lord's hands we commend your body and spirit.

Leader: The Lord will guard you
     from all harm; he will guard your life.
He guards you now, when you leave,
     and when you return.
Now and forever.

All: Into the Lord's hands we commend your body and spirit

Healings at Simon's House

Reading: Luke 4:38–40

After he left the synagogue, [Jesus] entered the house of Simon. Simon's mother-in-law was afflicted with a severe fever, and they interceded with him about her. He stood over her, rebuked the fever, and it left her. She got up immediately and waited on them. At sunset, all who had people sick with various diseases brought them to him. He laid his hands on each of them and cured them.

After the reading, each person present may come forward, place hands on the patient, and quietly pray for him or her.

Leader: We ask that the Lord lay his healing hands upon (name). May this time of surgery be filled with God's spirit and lead him/her to full health and recovery. We pray to the Lord:

All: Lord, lay your healing hands upon (name).

Leader: Lord, we pray for the surgeon and doctors. We ask you, Lord, to guide their hands skillfully. Watch over them through the course of the surgery and recovery. Let your healing power and peaceful presence be a part of every second of this time. We pray to the Lord:

All: Lord, lay your healing hands upon (name).

Leader: Lord, we pray for the nurses and the hospital staff. Let their gentle and loving care for (name) reflect your healing power and presence. We pray to the Lord:

All: Lord, lay your healing hands upon (name).

Leader: Lord, we pray for all of us, the family and friends of (name). Help us to rest our worry and to be filled with hope and trust. Lord, we know that you are the Divine Physician, one who will restore our friend back to health. We pray to the Lord:

All: Lord, lay your healing hands upon (name).

Leader: We now take time to add any of our personal petitions.

All: Lord, you have made (name) and brought him/her to this moment. Protect him/her as the surgery begins and be at his/her side during the course of the day. When the surgery is over, walk by his/her side to the recovery room. When he/she awakes, may your presence and peace be his/her first experience and remain with him/her in the days of healing to follow. We trust in your healing hands, O Lord, now and always! Amen.

BASED ON ISAIAH 43:1-4:

But now thus says the Lord,
Do not fear, for I have redeemed you;
I have called you by name,
you are mine.

When you pass through the waters,
I will be with you;
and through the rivers,
they shall not overwhelm you.

Because you are precious in my sight,
and honored, and I love you.

About the Author

It was after discovering the joy of a personal relationship with Jesus Christ that Pat Ritter decided to answer God's call to a life of service as a Catholic priest. Ordained in Seattle in 1974, Fr. Pat has served the people of seven parishes in the Seattle area for more than forty years.

The son of a railroad engineer and a maternity nurse, Fr. Pat is grateful for how the faith, love, and support of his parents shaped him into who he is today.

His parents also encouraged his love of music, and Fr. Pat still plays the piano and pipe organ with enthusiasm and joy. He loves nothing more than accompanying a sing-along. He has a popular tradition of playing Christmas carols on the pipe organ for the students at the parish schools where he has served.

Fr. Pat's joyful nature also shines through his quick wit and gift for storytelling, many times ending his tales with a hearty laugh and a disarmingly warm smile.

Fr. Pat hails from Vancouver, WA.

CPSIA information can be obtained
at www.ICGtesting.com
Printed in the USA
FFHW021151241118
49398696-53810FF